Hindi phrasebook

A Pilgrims Key to Hindi

Hindi phrasebook

A Pilgrims Key to Hindi

by
Paul Wanger

PILGRIMS PUBLISHING
◆ Varanasi ◆

Hindi Phrasebook
Paul Wanger

Published by:
PILGRIMS PUBLISHING

B 27/98 A-8, Nawabganj Road
Durga Kund, Varanasi-221010, India
Tel: 91-542- 2314060,
Fax: 91-542- 2312456
E-mail: pilgrims@satyam.net.in
Website: www.pilgrimsbooks.com

Edition

Edited by Christopher N Burchett
Layout & Cover design by Asha Mishra

ISBN: 81-7769-222-4

Printed in India at Pilgrim Press Pvt. Ltd. Lalpur Varanasi

Contents

Introduction

Travelling to India is a great chance to experience another way of life. Yet many tourists are not open-minded or knowledgeable enough to really appreciate the new and varied pleasures of India. Travelling is also a great way to make new acquaintances and friends, but communication can often be a problem. Learning some Hindi, India's most widely-spoken language, is an enjoyable way for the visitor to India to become more knowledgeable and to communicate better.

'But everyone speaks English in India!' Yes, quite a few from the middle class and the cities do. But many more Indians speak little or no English. With some knowledge of Hindi, you will be able to have simple conversations with fellow travellers on the train or bus, with traders in the market, with children in the street, with countrysiders… And you will receive lots of smiles for making the effort to speak the language.

Hindi is one of the world's great languages with more than 400 million speakers across much of northern and central India as well as many places where Indians have migrated such as the the United Kingdom, Fiji and the Caribbean. Urdu — a major language of Pakistan — is so similar to Hindi in its spoken form that you will be able to make yourself understood in Pakistan too.

Hindi is one of the easier foreign languages to learn. It belongs to the same family of languages as English: the Indo-European language family. So the basic grammatical structure of Hindi is not hugely different from that of English, French or German.

Ever since that early tourist, Alexander the Great, visited India in 327 BC, many foreigners have visited and lived in India. So it is not surprising that dozens of Hindi words have entered English (for example, *bungalow*, *dinghy*, *shampoo* and *jungle*).

Studying Hindi will help you understand the meaning of Indian culture — the food, religion, art, music and history — that you see all around when travelling in India. Maybe it will even help you to get into one of those blockbuster Hindi films!

So jump right in! Read the Hindi words and phrases aloud from the phrasebook. Ask Indian friends to read out the words and phrases for you to listen to and imitate. Use these words and phrases every day as you order a meal, as you visit the market or as you travel around. By spending just ten minutes a day on your Hindi study, you will experience rapid progress and soon enjoy the benefits.

Pronunciation

Hindi is written in a script called Devanagari but in this book we have represented the Hindi words and phrases with their closest Latin letter equivalents.

VOWELS

SHORT VOWELS

a	as the 'a' in 'ago'
e	as the 'e' in 'get'
i	as the 'i' in 'bit'
o	as the 'o' in 'on'
u	as the 'u' in 'put'

LONG VOWELS

ā	as the 'a' in 'father'
ē	as the 'ay' in 'day'
ī	as the 'ee' in 'see'
ō	as the 'o' in 'note'
ū	as the 'oo' in 'soon'
ai	as the 'a' in 'add'
au	as the 'au' in 'sauce'

CONSONANTS

b	as the 'b' in 'ball'
ch	as the 'ch' in 'church'
d	as the 'd' in 'dear'
f	as the 'f' in 'fan'
g	as the 'g' in 'give'
h	as the 'h' in 'hotel'
j	as the 'j' in 'jam'
k	as the 'k' in 'skin'

kh	as the 'k' in 'kite'
l	as the 'l' in 'lip'
m	as the 'm' in 'mud'
n	as the 'n' in 'now'
ng	as the 'ng' in 'wrong'
p	as the 'p' in 'pin'
ph	as the 'p' in 'photo'
r	as the 'r' in 'run'
s	as the 's' in 'see'
sh	as the 'sh' in 'she'
t	as the 't' in 'stop'
th	as the 't' in 'top' (*not* as the 'th' in 'theatre' or in 'the')
v	as the 'v' in 'vine'
w	as the 'w' in 'we'
y	as the 'y' in 'yes'
z	as the 'z' in 'zebra'

TWO OTHER POINTS

A dot under a letter (e.g. ḍ) means

that this letter is *aspirated* (or 'breathed') a little more than normally.

The letter 'ñ' indicates a preceding vowel that is *nasalised* (said through the nose). The 'n' itself is not pronounced. This is similar to the French word 'pardon', in which the vowel 'o' is nasalised by the following silent 'n'.

Grammar

WORD ORDER

The basic word order in a simple Hindi sentence is in the pattern:

Subject–Predicate–Verb.

e.g. (1) The room is big.
Kamrā barā hai.
(literally) Room big is.

e.g. (2) I will give ten rupees.
Maiñ das rupyē dūñgā.
(literally) I ten rupees will-give.

ARTICLES

Articles (*the*, *a* and *an*) are generally not used in Hindi.

e.g. (1) *Maiñ chātra hūñ.*
I am (a) student.

e.g. (2) *Mandir kahāñ hai?*
Where is (the) temple?

NOUNS

Nouns are either masculine or feminine in gender. Nouns ending in *a* are usually masculine; those ending in *i* are usually feminine.

e.g. *larkā* - boy; *larkī* - girl

Nouns are either singular or plural in number. The plural number is generally shown by adding a different suffix (ending).

e.g. *larkē* - boys; *larkiyāñ* - girls

ADJECTIVES

Adjectives are either masculine or feminine, singular or plural. They agree in gender and number with the nouns or pronouns they describe.

e.g.	*barā larkā*	big boy
	barē larkē	big boys
	barī larkī	big girl
	barī larkiyāñ	big girls

POSTPOSITIONS

In English words such as *in* or *to* are called *prepositions* and are placed before the nouns or pronouns which they govern. In Hindi the equivalent words are called *postpositions* and come after the nouns or pronouns they govern.

e.g. *Dillī mēñ* - in Delhi
mēz par - on the table

VERBS

An important verb you will meet often in Hindi is *hōnā* (to be). Its forms are irregular:

e.g.	*maiñ hūñ*	I am
	vah hai	he/she/it is
	āp haiñ	you are
	vē haiñ	they are

The infinitive of Hindi verbs ends in *nā*.
e.g. *bōlnā* to speak, say
(verb stem *bōl* + infinitive ending *nā*).

Hindi often expresses the present using the imperfective present tense (the verb stem ending in *tā*, *tī* or *tē*, depending on the gender and the number of the subject, followed by part of the verb *hōnā*).
e.g. *Maiñ jātā hūñ* I (masc.) go
(verb stem *ja* ending in masc. sing. ending *tā*, followed by *hūñ*)
Vah jātī hai She goes
Āp jātē haiñ You (plur.) go

The imperative ends in *ō*.
e.g. *āō!* - come!

There is also a polite form of the imperative which ends in *iyē*.
e.g. *āiyē!* - please come!

General Expressions

Hello.
Namastē.

How are you?
Āp kaisē haiñ?

Well, thank you.
Thīk hūñ, dhanyavād.

I beg your pardon.
Kshamā kījīyē.

You are welcome.
Āp kā svāgat hai.

What is your name?
Āp kā kyā nām hai?

My name is Peter Brown.
Mērā nām Peter Brown hai.

Where do you come from?
Āp kahāñ sē āyē haiñ?

I come from America.
Maiñ Amērika sē āyā hūñ.

I come from Australia.
Maiñ Astrēlīyā sē āyā hūñ.

I come from England.
Maiñ Ingēnd sē āyā hūñ.

I come from France.
Maiñ Frāns sē āyā hūñ.

I come from Germany.
Maiñ Jarmanī sē āyā hūñ.

I come from Japan.
Maiñ Jāpān sē āyā hūñ.

I come from Switzerland.
Maiñ Switzerlēnd sē āyā hūñ.

Please come in.
Kripyā undar āiyē.

Please sit down.
Kripyā baiṭh jāiyē.

Can you speak English?
Kyā āp Inglīsh bōl saktē haiñ?

Can you speak French?
Kyā āp Frēnch bōl saktē haiñ?

Can you speak German?
Kyā āp Jarman bōl saktē haiñ?

Can you speak Japanese?
Kyā āp Jāpānī bōl saktē haiñ?

Yes, a little.
Jī hāñ, kuchḥ kuchḥ.

I speak only a little Hindi.
Maiñ thorhi hindi bōl saktā hūñ.

Please speak slowly.
Kripyā dhirē bōliyē.

Please repeat.
Kripyā dōhrāiyē.

I am cold.
Mujhē sardī lug rahī hai.

I am frightened.
Maiñ ḍarā huā hūñ.

I am hot.
Mujhē garmī lug rahī hai.

I am hungry.
Maiñ bhūkhā hūñ.

I am thirsty.
Maiñ pyāsā hūñ.

Where is the American Embassy?
Amērikan Ēmbaissī kahāñ hai?

Where is the Australian Embassy?
Astrēlīyan Ēmbaissī kahāñ hai?

Where is the British Embassy?
British Ēmbaissī kahāñ hai?

Where is the French Embassy?
Frēnch Ēmbaissī kahāñ hai?

Where is the German Embassy?
Jarman Ēmbaissī kahāñ hai?

Where is the Japanese Embassy?
Japānī Ēmbaissī kahāñ hai?

Where is the Swiss Embassy?
Swiss Ēmbaissī kahāñ hai?

Where is the bank?
Bank kahāñ hai?

Where is the barber?
Nāī kahāñ hai?

Where is the immigration office?
Imigrēshion aufis kahāñ hai?

Where is the market?
Bāzār kahāñ hai?

Where is the mosque?
Masjid kahāñ hai?

Where is the police station?
Pulis chaukī kahāñ hai?

Where is the post office?
Dāk ghar kahāñ hai?

Where is the railway station?
Rēlwē stēshan kahāñ hai?

Where is the temple?
Mandir kahāñ hai?

Where is the toilet?
Shauchālay kahāñ hai?

Where is the tourist office?
Tūrist aufis kahāñ hai?

Please show me on this map.
Kripyā mujhē nakshē par dikhāiyē.

What street is this?
Yah kaun sī sarak hai?

Yes.
Jī hāñ.

No.
Jī nahīñ.

Maybe.
Shāyad.

What is this?
Yah kyā hai?

What is your occupation?
Āp kyā kartē haiñ?

I am a businessman.
Maiñ vyavasāyī hūñ.

I am a journalist.
Maiñ patrakār hūñ.

I am a musician.
Maiñ sañgītkār hūñ.

I am an office worker.
Maiñ daftar mēñ kām kartā hūñ.

I am a student.
Maiñ chātra hūñ.

I am a teacher.
Maiñ adhyāpak hūñ.

How old are you?
Āpkī kyā umrā haiñ?

I am 20 years old.
Maiñ bīs sāl kā hūñ.

Are you married?
Kyā āp shādishudā haiñ?

Yes, I am married.
Jī hāñ, maiñ shādīshudā hūñ.

I have two children.
Mērē dō bachchē haiñ.

Not yet.
Abhī nahīñ.

Thank you.
Dhanyavād.

Please accept this small gift.
Kripyā yah chōtā sā uphār swīkār kijīyē.

Please accept this tip.
Kripyā yah bakshish svīkār kijīyē.

Here is my name card.
Yē hai mērā parīchaya patra.

Goodbye.
Namastē.

Who?
Kaun?

What?
Kyā?

Where?
Kahāñ?

When?
Kab?

Why?
Kyōñ?

How?
Kaisē?

How much?
Kitnā?

How many?
Kitnē?

Accommodation

Where is the hotel?
Hōtal kahāñ hai?

Do you have a single room?
Kyā āpkē pās ēk vyakti kē thaharnē kā kamrā hai?

Do you have a double room?
Kyā āpkē pās do vyaktiyoñ kē thaharnē kā kamrā hai?

I need just a dormitory bed.
Maiñ bas ēk dormitorī chāhta hūñ.

Is a bathroom attached?

Snāngrah sāth mēñ hai?

Have you an air-conditioned room?

Kyā āpkē pās ēr kondishand kamrā hai?

What is the rent for one day?

Ēk din kā kyā kirāyā hai?

Can I see the room?

Kyā maiñ kamrā dēkh saktā huñ?

I need a better room.

Mujhē adhik achchā kamrā chāhīyē.

I need a cheaper room.
Mujḥē adhik sastā kamrā chāhīyē.

I need a quieter room.
Mujḥē adhik shāntipurna kamrā chāhīyē.

I need a cleaner room.
Mujḥē adhik safsutḥrā kamrā chāhīyē.

This room is too small.
Yah bahut cḥōtā kamrā hai.

This room is too big.
Yah bahut barḥā kamrā hai.

I need hot water.
Mujḥē garam pānī chāhīyē.

I need ice.
Mujḥē barf chāhīyē.

I need a mosquito net.
Mujḥē macḥardānī chāhīyē.

I need a lamp.
Mujhē batī chāhīyē.

I need a pillow.
Mujḥē takīyā chāhīyē.

I need a towel.
Mujḥē tauliyā chāhīyē.

I need soap.
Mujḥē sābun chāhīyē.

I need toilet paper.
Mujhē shauch kā kāgaz chāhīyē.

I need a sheet.
Mujḥē chādar chāhīyē.

I need a blanket.
Mujḥē kambal chāhīyē.

I need another blanket.
Mujḥē ēk aur kambal chāhīyē.

I need a fan.
Mujḥē pankhā chāhīyē.

I need a lock.
Mujḥē tālā chāhīyē.

I need a key.
Mujḥē chābhī chāhīyē.

I need a bulb.
Mujḥē bulb chāhīyē.

Is there a telephone?

Kyā yahāñ tēlīfōn hai?

Is there a laundry service?

Kyā yahāñ kapdē dhulne kī suvidhā hai?

Is there breakfast?

Kyā nāshtā hai?

I want to speak to the manager.

Maiñ prabandhak sē bāt karna chāhtā hūñ.

Please wake me at 7 am.

Kripyā mujḥē subah sāt bajē utḥāiyē.

I am leaving tomorrow.

Maiñ kal jā rahā hūñ.

Here is my new address.

Yah mērā nayā patā hai.

Please forward my mail.

Kripyā mērē patra bhēj dījiyē.

I shall return tomorrow.

Maiñ kal vāpas aūñgā.

Please call a taxi.

Kripyā taiksī bulvā dījiyē.

Food

Where is a good restaurant?
Achchā bhojanālay kahāñ hai?

May I see the menu?
Kyā maiñ menyū dēkh saktā hūñ?

Please give me lentil soup.
Kripyā mujḥē dāl kā shōrbā chāhīyē.

Please give me a plate of rice.
Kripyā mujḥē ēk thālī chāval dījīyē.

Please give me a sandwich.
Kripyā mujḥē sandvich dījīyē.

Please give me a cup of tea.
Kripyā mujḥē ēk pyālā chāy dījīyē.

Please give me a glass of water.
Kripyā mujḥē ēk gīlās pānī dījīyē.

Please give me a bottle of beer.
Kripyā ēk bīr kī bōtal dījīyē.

Please bring a cup.
Kripyā ēk pyālā lāīyē.

Please bring a plate.
Kripyā ēk thāli lāīyē.

Please bring a glass.
Kripyā ēk gilās lāīyē.

Please bring a knife.
Kripyā ēk chākū lāiye.

Please bring a spoon.
Kripyā ēk chammach lāīyē.

Please bring a fork.
Kripyā ēk kānta lāīyē.

Please bring pepper.
Kripyā mirch lāīyē.

Please bring salt.
Kripyā namak lāīyē.

I don't eat spicy food.
Maiñ masālēdār khānā nahīñ khātā hūñ.

I don't eat eggs.
Maiñ andē nahīñ khātā hūñ.

I don't eat meat.
Maiñ māñs nahīñ khātā hūñ.

I did not order this.
Maiñe yē nahīñ māngvāyā thā.

Please bring me the bill.
Kripyā bill sūchī lāīyē.

Fruit. *Phal.*

Banana. *Kēlā.*

Coconut. *Nārīyal*

Lemon. *Nīmbū.*

Mango.	*Ām.*
Vegetables.	*Sabẓīyāñ.*
Lentils.	*Dālēñ.*
Peas.	*Maṭar.*
Potato.	*Ālū.*
Spinach.	*Pālak.*
Butter.	*Makkhan.*
Vegetable patties.	*Sabẓī kā samōsā.*
Cheese.	*Panīr.*
Curd.	*Dahī.*

Milk.	*Dūdh.*
Eggs.	*Andē.*
Meat.	*Māñs.*
Mutton.	*Bạkrē kā māñs.*
Chicken.	*Murgī.*
Rice.	*Chāval.*
Bread.	*Rōtī.*
Unleavened bread.	*Chapātī.*
Vegetable curry.	*Rasedār sabẓī.*

Lamb curry.	*Bhēṛh kā rasedār māñs.*
Mince.	*Kīma.*
Non-vegetable curry.	*Kōrmā.*
Meat balls.	*Māñs kōftā.*
Stuffed pancake.	*Masālā dōsā.*
Sweets.	*Mīthāīyāñ.*
Semolina balls in rose syrup.	*Gulāb jāmun.*
Water.	*Pānī.*

Boiled water.	*Ublā pānī.*
Cold water.	*Ṭhandā pānī.*
Tea.	*Chāi.*
Coffee.	*Kaufī.*
With milk.	*Dūdḥ kē sāṭḥ.*
With sugar.	*Chīnī kē sāth.*

Time and Numbers

What is the time?
Kyā samay hai?

It is six o'clock.
Chhē bajē haiñ.

It is six o'clock in the morning.
Subah kē chhē bajē haiñ.

It is six o'clock in the evening.
Shām kē chhē bajē haiñ.

It is 6.15.
Savā chhē haiñ.

It is 6.30.
Sārhē chhē haiñ.

It is 6.45.
Paunē sāt haiñ.

It is 6.10.
Chhē baj kar das mīnat haiñ.

It is 6.50.
Sāt bajnē mēñ das mīnat haiñ.

It is 12 noon.
Dopahar kē bārah bajē haiñ.

It is 12 midnight.
Rāt kē bārah bajē haiñ.

Now. *Ab.*

Today. *Āj.*

This week. *Yah saptāh.*

Yesterday.	*Kal.*
Last week.	*Pichhlē saptāh.*
Tomorrow.	*Kal.*
The day after tomorrow.	*Parsoñ.*
Next week.	*Aglē saptāh.*
1.	*Ēk.*
2.	*Dō.*
3.	*Tīn.*
4.	*Chār.*
5.	*Pānch.*

6.	*Chhē.*
7.	*Sāt.*
8.	*Āṭh.*
9.	*Nau.*
10.	*Das.*
11.	*Gyārā.*
12.	*Bārā.*
13.	*Tērā.*
14.	*Chaudā.*
15.	*Pandrā.*

16.	Sōlā.
17.	*Sattarā.*
18.	*Athārā.*
19.	*Unnīs.*
20.	*Bīs.*
30.	*Tīs.*
40.	*Chālīs.*
50.	*Pachās.*
60.	*Sāth.*
70.	*Sattar.*

80.	*Assī.*
90.	*Nabbē.*
100.	Ēk sau.
200.	*Dō sau.*
300.	*Tīn sau.*
1000.	*Ēk hazār.*

Transportation

Where is the railway station?
Rēlwē stēshan kahāñ hai?

Where is the bus stop?
Bas addā kahāñ hai?

Where is the bus station?
Bas stēshan kahāñ hai?

Where is the ticket office?
Tikat ghar kahāñ hai?

Where is the airport?
Havāī addā kahāñ hai?

How far?
Kitnī dūr?

When will the bus leave?
Bas kab chalēgī?

When will the train leave?
Trēn kab chalēgī?

How much is the ticket to Delhi?
Delhi kā tikat kitnē kī hai?

I would like a ticket to Calcutta.
Mujhē Kalkatta kā tikat chāhīyē.

I would like two tickets to Calcutta.
Mujhē Kalkatta kē dō tikatē chāhīyē.

First class.
Prāṭhạm sharēṇī.

Second class.
Dūsrī sharēṇī.

Third class.
Tisrī sharēṇī.

I would like a sleeper.
Maiñ slīpar chāhūnga.

Is this the train to Agra?
Kyā yah trēn Agra kī hai?

Is this an express train?
Kyā yah tēzgāmi gārḥi hai?

Where is the dining car?
Bhōjanyān kahāñ hai?

Is this seat free?
Kyā yah jagah khālī hai?

Please tell me when we come to Varanasi.
Kripyā batāīyē ham Vārānāsi kab āyēñ.

How long does this train stop here?
Yah trēn yahāñ kabtak rukēgi?

Take my luggage to a taxi.
Merā sāmān taiksī mēñ lē jaiyē.

Which bus goes to Lucknow?
Kaun si bas Luknō jātī hai?

How much is the fare?
Kitnā kīrāyā hai?

When will the bus leave?
Bas kab chalēgi?

I want to go to the temple.
Maiñ mandīr jānā chāhtā hūñ.

How much?
Kitnā?

Drive quickly.
Jaldī chalāīyē.

Drive slowly.
Dhīrē chalāīyē.

Turn left.
Bāīñ taraf murḥiyē.

Turn right.
Dāhīnī taraf murḥiyē.

Straight.
Sīdhā.

Stop here.
Yahāñ rukīyē.

Can you wait for me?
Kyā āp mērā intzār kar saktē haiñ?

How much does the taxi to the airport cost?
Havāī addē tak taiksī mēñ jānē kā kītnā kirāyē lagēgā?

Post Office

Where is the post office?
Dāk ghar kahāñ hai?

May I have some postage stamps?
Kyā maiñ kucḥ dāk tikat lē saktā hūñ?

May I have some envelopes?
Kyā maiñ kucḥ lifāfē lē saktā hūñ?

May I have some aerogrammes?
Kyā maiñ kucḥ aerogram lē saktā hūñ?

May I have some postcards?
Kyā maiñ kuch̤ pōstkārd lē saktā hūñ?

I want three aerogrammes please.
Mujh̤ē tīn aerogram chāhīyē.

I want two 50 paise stamps please.
Mujh̤ē dō pachhās paisē vālī dāk tikatē chāhīyē.

I want to send this airmail.
Maiñ yah havāī dāk sē bhējnā chāhtā hūñ.

I want to send this express.
Maiñ yah ekspres dāk sē bhējnā chāhtā hūñ.

I want to send this registered.
Maiñ yah rejisterd dāk sē bhējnā chāhtā hūñ.

I want to send this insured.
Maiñ yah surkshit dāk sē bhējnā chāhtā hūñ.

This parcel contains printed matter.
Īs pārsal mēñ līkhīt sāmagrī hai.

This parcel contains personal belongings.
Īs pārsal mēñ nizi chīzēñ haiñ.

How much will it cost?
Iska kitnā kharch lagēgā?

Please give me a receipt.

Kripyā mujhē rasīd dījīyē.

Where can I mail this?

Maiñ yah kahāñ pōst kar saktā hūñ?

Have you received mail for Peter Brown?

Kyā āpkō Peter Brown kī dāk mil gai hai?

Bank

Where is the bank?
Bank kahāñ hai?

I want to change money.
Maiñ paisē bhunvānā chāhtā hūñ.

I want to change travellers cheques.
Maiñ travelers chēks bhunvānā chāhtā hūñ.

I want to change US dollars.
Maiñ US dollars bhunvānā chāhtā hūñ.

I want to change British pounds.
Maiñ Inglīsh pound bhunvānā chāhtā hūñ.

I want to change German marks.
Maiñ Jarman marks bhunvānā chāhtā hūñ.

What is the exchange rate for French francs?
Frēnch franks kā kyā vīnīmay dar hai?

What is the exchange rate for Swiss francs?
Swiss franks kā vīnīmay dar kyā hai?

I want a cash advance on my credit card.

Maiñ apnē kredit kārd sē udhār lēnā chāhtā hūñ.

Please change this into smaller notes (bills).

Kripyā isē chotē rupaiyōñ mēñ badal dījiyē.

Please change this into coins.

Kripyā yah sikkoñ mēñ badal dījiyē.

Health

Where is a doctor?
Doktur kahāñ hai?

Where is a dentist?
Dāñtoñ kā doktur kahāñ hai?

Where is a hospital?
Aspatāl kahāñ hai?

Where is a pharmacy?
Kemist kahāñ hai?

Where is an ayurvedic doctor?
Āyūrvēdik doktur kahāñ hai?

Where is a unani doctor?
Unāni doktur kahāñ hai?

I am sick.
Maiñ bīmār hūñ.

Please get me a doctor at once.
Kripyā doktor kō jaldī bulvāīyē.

I have a cold.
Mujhē zukām hai.

I have a fever.
Mujhē bukhār hai.

I have diarrhoea.
Mujhē atīsār hai.

My stomach hurts.
Mērē pēt mēñ dard hai.

My chest hurts.
Mērē sīnẹ mēñ dard hai.

My back hurts.
Mērī pīṭh mēñ dard hai.

It hurts here.
Yahāñ dard hai.

I can't eat.
Maiñ khā nahīñ saktā.

I can't sleep.
Maiñ sō nahīñ saktā.

I am constantly vomiting.
Mujḥē lagātār ultiyāñ hō rahī haiñ.

I have been sick for three days.
Maiñ pichḷē tīn dīnoñ sē bīmār hūñ.

I am tired.
Maiñ tḥakā hūñ.

My leg is broken.
Mērī tāng tūtī huī hai.

Is it broken?
Kyā yah tūt gaī hai?

Is it serious?
Kyā yah gambhīr hai?

Arm. *Bāzū.*

Back. *Pīṭḥ.*

Blood.	*Khūn.*
Bone.	*Haḍḍī.*
Breast.	*Cḥātī.*
Cheek.	*Gāl.*
Chest.	*Sīnā.*
Ear.	*Kān.*
Eye.	*Āñkh.*
Face.	*Chēhrā.*
Finger.	*Ūnglī.*
Foot.	*Pair.*

Hand.	*Hāth.*
Head.	*Sir.*
Heart.	*Dil.*
Kidney.	*Gurdā.*
Leg.	*Tāng.*
Liver.	*Jīgar.*
Nose.	*Nāk.*
Shoulder.	*Kandhā.*
Stomach.	*Pēt.*
Throat.	*Galā.*

Tongue.	*Jībh.*
Tooth.	*Dāñt.*
Asthma.	*Damā.*
Cholera.	*Hēẓā.*
Cold.	*Sardī zukām.*
Condom	*Kondom.*
Constipation.	*Kabẓ.*
Cramps.	*Eñṭhan.*
Diarrhoea.	*Dast.*
Dysentery.	*Pēchish.*

Fever.	*Bukhār.*
Headache.	*Sir dard.*
Hepatitis.	*Pīliyā.*
Indigestion.	*Apach.*
Malaria.	*Malēriā.*
Menstruation.	*Mahāvārī.*
Rabies.	*Jalāntak.*
Tetanus.	*Tētnas.*
Typhoid.	*Āntrajavar.*
Pills.	*Gōlīyāñ.*

Prescription. *Doktur kā nuskhā.*

Give me some aspirin.
Mujḥē kuchḥ esprīn dījīyē.

Give me some antiseptic cream.
Mujḥē kuchḥ antīsēptik krīm dījīyē.

Give me some disinfectant.
Mujḥē kuchḥ disinfektant dījīyē.

Give me some cough drops.
Mujḥē kuch khānsī kī davā dījīyē.

Give me some eye drops.
Mujḥē koi āñkh mēñ dālnē ki davā dījīyē.

Give me some sleeping pills.
Mujḥē kucḥ sōnē kī gōlīyāñ dījīyē.

How many times a day?
Dīn mēñ kitnī bār?

Three times a day.
Dīn mēñ tīn bār.

I'm allergic to penicillin.
Maiñ pēnisilīn sē ēlargīk hūñ.

How much is this per tablet?
Īs ēk gōlī kī kyā kīmat hai?

Please buy medicine for me at the pharmacy.
Kripyā davā kī dukān sē mērē liyē ōshdhī kharīd lē.

What is this medicine?
Yah kauṇ sī davā hai?

Burn.	*Jalnā.*
Itch.	*Khūjalī.*
Pain.	*Dard.*
Injection.	*Tīkā.*
Test.	*Jāñch.*

Shopping

Where is the shop?
Dukān kahāñ hai?

Where is the market?
Bāẕār kaḥāñ ḥai?

Where is the pharmacy?
Oshdhi vīkrēta kahāñ hai?

Where is the tailor?
Darzī kahāñ hai?

Where is the barber?
Nāī kahāñ hai?

Where is the bookshop?
Kitābōñ kī dukān kahāñ hai?

How much?
Kitnā?

That is too expensive.
Yah bahut māhēngā hai.

The quality is not good.
Yah achchī nahīñ hai.

Do you have something cheaper?
Kyā āpkē pās kuch aur sastā hai?

What is your lowest price?
Āpka kam sē kam kyā dām hai?

I will give you 100 rupees.
Maiñ āpkō sau rupaiyē dūñgā.

That's OK.
Yē thīk hai.

I will take it.
Maiñ lē luñgā.

I do not want that.
Mujḥē vah nahīñ chāhīyē.

That is too big.
Vah bahut barā hai.

That is too small.
Vah bahut cḥōtā hai.

That is too long.
Vah bahut lambā hai.

That is too short.
Vah bahut cḥōtā hai.

That is too tight.
Vah bahut tang hai.

That is too loose.
Vah bahut dḥīlā hai.

That is too much.
Vah bahut zyādā hai.

That is enough.
Vah kāfī hai.

That is not enough.
Vah kāfī nahīñ hai.

Can I see that?
Kyā maiñ dēkh saktā hūñ?

Please show me another style.
Mujḥē koi dusarī tarah kā dikhāīyē.

Please show me another colour.
Mujḥē dusarā rañg dikhāīyē.

Do you have any more?
Āpkē pās kuch aur hai?

Red. *Lāl.*

Blue. *Nīlā.*

Yellow. *Pīlā.*

Green. *Harā.*

Brown. *Bḥūrā.*

Grey. *Salētī.*

White. *Safēd.*

Black. *Kālā.*

How much does this cost?
Yah kitnē kā hai?

How much does this shirt cost?
Yē kamīz kitnē kī hai?

How much does one kilogramme cost?
Ēk kilō kā kyā dām hai?

How much does one metre cost?
Ēk mītar kitnē kā hai?

How much does one (piece) cost?
Ēk tukrḥā kitnē kā hai?

Do you have soap?
Kyā āpkē pās sābun hai?

Do you have a comb?
Kyā āpkē pās kanghī hai?

Do you have mosquito repellent?
Kyā āpkē pās machrōñ kō bhagānē kī davā hai?

Do you have matches?
Kyā āpkē pās diyāsalāi hai?

Do you have string?
Kyā āpkē pās rassī hai?

Do you have needle and thread?
Kyā āpkē pās sūī dḥāgā hai?

Do you have buttons?
Kyā āpkē pās batan haiñ?

Do you have paper?
Kyā āpkē pās kāgaz hai?

Do you have pens?
Kyā āpkē pās kalam hai?

Do you have envelopes?
Kyā āpkē pās lifāfē haiñ?

Do you have newspapers?
Kyā āpkē pās akhbār hai?

Do you have maps?
Kyā āpkē pās nakshē haiñ?

Do you have film?
Kyā āpkē pās film hai?

I want a book.
Mujhē kitāb chāhīyē.

I want a packet of cigarettes.
Mujhē ēk paket sigrēṭ chāhīyē.

I want a pair of trousers.
Mujhē patlūn chāhīyē.

I want a skirt.
Mujhē skārṭ chāhīyē.

I want a shirt.
Mujhē kamīz chāhīyē.

I want some shoes.
Mujhē kuchḥ jūtē chāhīyē.

I want some socks.
Mujhē kuchḥ mōzē chāhīyē.

I want shoe laces.
Mujhē fītē chāhīyē.

I want jewellery.
Mujḥē zēvar chāhīyē.

I want an umbrella.
Mujḥē cḥatrī chāhīyē.

Do you accept travellers cheques?
Kyā āp travelers chēks manzōr kartē haiñ?

Do you accept credit cards?
Kyā āp kredit kārds manzōr kaṛtē haiñ?

Sightseeing

I need a tour guide.
Mujḥē tūr gāid chāhīyē.

I do not need a tour guide.
Mujḥē tūr gāid nahīñ chāhīyē.

I wish to see the main sights.
Maiñ yahāñ kē vishēsh darshnīya sthān dēkhnā chāhta hūñ.

I have one day for sightseeing.
Mērē pās darshnīya sthān dēkhnē kē liyē ēk din hai.

I have half a day for sightseeing.
Mērē pās darshnīya sthān dēkhnē kē liyē ādhā din hai.

I have two days for sightseeing.
Mērē pās darshnīya sthān dēkhnē kē liyē dō din haiñ.

Are you a registered tour guide?
Kyā āp rejisterd tūr gāid haiñ?

How much do you charge per day?
Āp ēk din kē kitnē paisē lētē haiñ?

I wish to see the temple.
Maiñ mandir dēkhnā chāhtā hūñ.

I wish to see the mosque.
Maiñ masjid dēkhnā chāhtā hūñ.

I wish to see the monastery.
Maiñ maṭh dēkhna chāhtā huñ.

I wish to see the palace.
Maiñ mahal dēkhnā chāhtā hūñ.

I wish to see the fort.
Maiñ kilā dēkhnā chāhtā hūñ.

I wish to see the park.
Maiñ park dēkhnā chāhtā hūñ.

I wish to see the botanic gardens.
Maiñ vanaspati bāg dēkhnā chāhtā hūñ.

I wish to see the museum.
Maiñ myūzīam dēkhnā chāhtā hūñ.

I wish to see the art gallery.
Maiñ kalā pradarshani dēkhnā chāhtā hūñ.

I wish to see the parliament.
Maiñ sansad bhavan dēkhnā chāhtā hūñ.

I wish to see the Old City.
Maiñ purānā shahēr dēkhnā chāhtā hūñ.

I wish to see some handicraft shops.
Maiñ kuchḥ dastkārī kī dukānē dēkhnā chāhtā hūñ.

I wish to see the main street.
Maiñ mukhya sarak dēkhnā chāhtā hūñ.

I wish to see the back streets.
Maiñ pīchē kī galīyañ dēkhnā chāhtā hūñ.

I wish to see the river.
Maiñ nadī dēkhnā chāhtā hūñ.

I wish to see the lake.
Maiñ jhīl dēkhnā chāhtā hūñ.

I wish to see the mountain.
Maiñ pahārḥ dēkhnā chāhtā hūñ.

I wish to see the caves.
Maiñ gufāēñ dēkhnā chāhtā hūñ.

I wish to see the beach.
Maiñ samudra taṭ dēkhnā chāhtā hūñ.

I wish to see an Indian film.
Maiñ Bhārtiy film dēkhnā chāhtā hūñ.

I wish to hear Indian music.
Maiñ Bhārtiy sangīt sunanā chāhtā hūñ.

I wish to learn yoga.
Maiñ yōgā sīkhnā chāhtā hūñ

I wish to see the Indian cricket team.
Maiñ Bhārtiy krikēt tīm dēkhnā chāhtā hūñ.

Can we take a taxi?
Kyā ham taiksī lē saktē haiñ?

Can we take a rickshaw?
Kyā ham rikshā lē saktē haiñ?

Can we take a boat?
Kyā ham nāv lē saktē haiñ?

Can we rest for ten minutes?
Kyā ham das minat kē liyē arām kar saktē haiñ?

Can we take refreshments?
Kyā ham jalpān lē saktē haiñ?

Can we eat now?
Kyā ham ab khā saktē haiñ?

I want to leave here now.
Maiñ ab yahāñ sē jānā chātā hūñ.

I want to return to my hotel now.
Maiñ apnē hōtal abhī vāpas jāṇā chātā hūñ.

I will pay you now.
Maiñ abhī tumhē paisē dūñgā.

Here is a tip.
Yah inām hai.

You are a good guide.
Āp achchē gāid haiñ.

Thank you very much.
Āpkā bahut dhanyavād.

Can I see you again tomorrow?

Kyā maiñ kal āpse mil saktā hūñ?

Can I see you again tomorrow at 8 am?

Kyā maiñ āpse kal subh āṭh bajē mil saktā hūñ?

Trekking

Will you go with me?
Āp mērē sāth chalēñgē?

I have to go to Zanskar.
Mujḥē Zanskār jānā haiñ.

How many days will it take?
Kitnē din lagēñgē?

What do you charge per day?
Āp ēk din kē kitnē paisē lētē haiñ?

With food. *Khānē kē sāth.*

Without food. *Binā khānē kē.*

With a load. *Bhār kē sāth.*

With a horse. *Ghōrhē kē sāth.*

With a mule. *Khachhar kē sāth.*

We will leave at six o'clock tomorrow morning.
Ham kal subh kē chhē bajē ravānā hōngē.

We will meet at this hotel.
Ham is hōtal mēñ milēñgē.

Which is the way to Rudranath?
Rudrānath kā kaun sā rāstā hai.

How many hours?
Kitnē ghantē?

How many days?
Kitnē din?

What is the next village?
Aglā kaun sā gaoñ hai?

North. *Uttar.*

South. *Dakshiṇ.*

East. *Pūrav.*

West. *Pashchim.*

On the left. *Bāiñ taraf.*

On the right. *Dāyēñ taraf.*

Near. *Pās.*

Far. *Dūr.*

This side. *Is taraf.*

That side. *Us taraf.*

Uphill. *Ūpar.*

Downhill. *Dḥalān.*

On this level. *Is satah par.*

Is there a place to spend the night?
Kyā rāt bītānē kī jagah hai?

Is food available?
Kyā bhōjan milegā?

Is water available?
Kyā pānī milegā?

I will pay.

Maiñ paisē dūñgā.

How much?

Kitnā?

Please ask about food.

Kripyā khānē kē bārē mēñ pūcḥēñ.

Please ask about tea.

Kripyā chāi kē bārē mēñ pūcḥēñ.

Please ask about bread.

Kripyā rōṭī kē bārē mēñ pūcḥēñ.

Please ask about boiled water.

Kripyā ublē pānī kē bārē mēñ pūcḥēñ.

Please give me cooked rice.
Kripyā mujḥē pakē huē chāval dījīyē.

Please give me vegetables.
Kripyā mujḥē sabẓīyāñ dījīyē.

Please give me tea.
Kripyā mujḥē chāy dījīyē.

Please give me shelter.
Kripyā mujḥē sharaṇ dījīyē.

Where is the bridge?
Pūl kahāñ hai?

Where is the inn?
Dharamshālā kahāñ hai?

Where is a resting place?
Arām kī jagah kahāñ hai?

Where is the teashop?
Chāy kī dukān kahāñ hai?

Where is the statue?
Pratimā kahāñ hai?

Where is the village?
Gaoñ kahāñ hai?

Do you have a basket?
Kyā āpkē pās tōkrī hai?

Do you have a bag?
Kyā āpkē pās thēlā hai?

Do you have a knife?
Kyā āpkē pās chākū hai?

Do you have firewood?
Kyā āpkē pās jalānē kī lakrī hai?

How far is the hill?
Pahārī kitnī dūr hai?

How far is the mountain?
Pahār kitnī dūr hai?

How far is the peak?
Chōti kitnī dūr hai?

How far is the forest?
Jangal kitnī dūr hai?

How far is the lake?
Jhīl kitnī dūr hai?

How far is the river?
Nadī kitnī dūr hai?

How far is the spring?
Jharanā kitnī dūr hai?

How far is the waterfall?
Jal prapāt kitnī dūr hai?

Today it is hot.
Āj garamī hai.

Today it is cold.
Āj sardī hai.

Will it be cloudy tomorrow?
Kyā kal bādal chāyē rahēñgē?

Will it be foggy tomorrow?
Kyā kal dhūndh hōgī?

Will it be rainy tomorrow?
Kyā kal barsāt hōgī?

Will it be sunny tomorrow?
Kyā kal dhūp hōgī?

Will it be humid tomorrow?
Kyā kal namī hōgī?

Will it be windy tomorrow?
Kyā kal havā hōgī?

Will it be good weather tomorrow?
Kyā kal achchā mausam hōgā?

Will it be bad weather tomorrow?
Kyā kal burā mausam hai?

Will there be thunder tomorrow?
Kyā kal bādal garjēñgē?

Will there be frost tomorrow?
Kyā kal pālā paṛhēga?

Will there be snow tomorrow?
Kyā kal barf parhēgī?

Bird. *Pakshī.*

Cow. *Gāi.*

Dog. *Kuttā.*

Monkey. *Bandar.*

Mosquito. *Machhar.*

Please come here.
Kripyā yahāñ āiyē.

Am I allowed to camp here?
Kyā maiñ yahāñ par shivir dāl saktā hūñ?

Where is the toilet?
Shōchālay kahāñ hai?

I have to rest.
Mujhē arām karnā hai.

Slowly.	*Dhīrē.*
Backpack.	*Pīth par latkānē kā thēlā.*
Candle.	*Mōmbattī.*
Kerosene.	*Miṭṭī kā tēl.*
Map.	*Nakshā.*
Matches.	*Māchīs.*

Sleeping bag.	*Sōnē kā thēlā.*
Stove.	Angīthī.
Tent.	*Tambū.*

Emergencies

Help!
Madad kījiyē.

Police!
Pulis! Pụlis!

Thief!
Chōr! chōr!

Danger!
Khạtrā!

Get help quickly!
Kripyā jaldī sahāyta bulvāyēn!

There has been an accident.
Vahāñ durghatnā hō gai hai.

I'm lost.
Maiñ rāstā bhūl gayā hūñ.

I have lost my passport.
Mērā pāspōrt gum hō gayā hai.

My camera was stolen.
Mērā kaimrā chōrī hō gayā hai.

My money was stolen.
Mērē paisē chōrī hō gayē haiñ.

Vocabulary

A

accident	*durghatnā*
aerogramme	*aerogram*
air conditioned	*ēr kondishand*
airmail	*havāī dāk*
airport	*havāī addā*
all right! OK!	*achchā!*
allergic	*ēlargīk*
always	*hamēshā*
America	*Amērika*
American	*Amērikan*
another (adj)	*aur*
antiseptic cream	*antīsēptik krīm*
are (eg they are)	*haiñ*
arm	*bāẓū*
art gallery	*kalā pradarshanī*
aspirin	*esprīn*

asthma	*damā*
Australia	*Astrēlīyā*
Australian	*Astrēlīyan*
available	*prāpt*

B

back (part of body)	*pīth*
back street	*pīchē kī sarak*
backpack	*pīth par latkānē kā thēlā*
bad	*burā*
bag	*thēlā*
banana	*kēlā*
bank	*bank*
barber	*nāī*
basket	*tōkrī*
bathroom	*snāngrah*
be, to	*hōnā*
be able to, to	*saknā*
beach	*samudra tat*

bed	*bistar*
beer	*bīr*
better	*adhik achchā*
big	*barā*
bill (restaurant)	*bill*
bill (paper money)	*nōt*
bird	*pakshī*
black	*kālā*
blanket	*kambal*
blood	*khūn*
blue	*nīlā*
boat	*nāv*
boiled water	*ublā pānī*
bone	*haddi*
book	*kitāb*
bookshop	*kitābōn ki dukān*
botanical gardens	*vanaspati bāg*
bread	*rōtī*
bread, unleavened	*chapātī*
breakfast	*nāshtā*

breast	*chāṭī*
bridge	*pūl*
bring, to	*lānā*
British	*Briṭish*
broken	*ṭūṭī*
brown	*bhūrā*
bulb, light	*bulb*
burn, to	*jalnā*
businessman	*vyavasāyī*
bus station	*bas stēshan*
bus stop	*bas addā*
butter	*makkhan*
button	*battun*

C

call, to	*bulānā*
camera	*kaimrā*
camp, to	*shivir dālnā*
candle	*mōmbattī*
cash advance	*udhār*

cave	*gūfā*
charge (money), to	*paisē lēnā*
cheap (inexpensive)	*sastā*
cheek	*gāl*
cheese	*panīr*
chemist (pharmacist)	*kemist*
chest	*sīnā*
chicken	*murgī*
cholera	*hēzā*
cigarette	*sigrēṭ*
clean (adj)	*sāf*
cloud	*bādal*
coconut	*nāriyal*
coffee	*kaufī*
coins	*sikkē*
cold (temperature)	*thandā*
cold (ailment)	*zukām*
colour	*rañg*
comb (n)	*kanghī*
come, to	*ānā*

condom	*kondom*
constantly (always)	*hamēshā*
constipation	*kabz*
cough drops	*khānsī kī davā*
cow	*gāi*
cramps	*eñṭhan*
credit card	*kredit kārd*
cricket	*krikēt*
cricket team	*krikēt tīm*
cup	*pyālā*
curd	*dahī*
curry	*rasedār sabzī*
curry, lamb	*bhērḥ kē māñs kī rasedār sabzī*
curry, non-vegetable	*kōrmā*
curry, vegetable	*rasedār sabzī*

D

danger	*khatrā*
day	*din*

day after tomorrow	*parsoñ*
dentist	*dāñtoñ kā doktur*
diarrhoea	*dast*
dining car	*bhōjanyān*
disinfectant	*disinfektant*
doctor	*doktur*
doctor, ayurvedic	*āyūrvēdik doktur*
doctor, unani	*unāni doktur*
dog	*kuttā*
dollar	*dollar*
dormitory	*dormitorī*
double room	*dō vyaktiyon kē ṭhaharnē kā kamrā*
downhill	*ḍhalān*
drive (a vehicle), to	*chalānā*
dysentery	*pēchish*

E

ear	*kān*
east	*pūrav*

eat, to	*khānā*
egg	*andā*
eight	*āṭh*
eighteen	*aṭhārā*
eighty	*assī*
eleven	*gyārā*
embassy	*ēmbaissī*
England	*Inglēnd*
English	*Inglish*
enough	*kāfī; bas*
envelope	*lifāfā*
evening	*shām*
exchange rate	*vinīmay dar*
expensive	*mahēñgā*
eye	*āñkh*
eye drops	*āñkh mē dālnē ki davā*

F

face	*chēhrā*

fan	*pankhā*
far (adj)	*dūr*
far, how?	*kitnī dūr?*
fever	*bukhār*
fifteen	*pandrā*
fifty	*pachās*
film (camera)	*film*
film (movie)	*film*
fine (good)	*thīk*
finger	*unglī*
firewood	*jalānē kī lakrhī*
first class (rail travel)	*prāthạm shrēṇī*
five	*pāṇch*
fog	*kōrhā*
food	*khānā*
foot (part of body)	*pair*
fork	*kāntā*
fort	*kilā*
forty	*chālīs*
forward (mail), to	*bhējnā*

four	*chār*
fourteen	*chaudā*
franc, French (currency)	*French frank*
France	*Frāns*
free (seat) (adj)	*khālī*
French	*Frēnch*
frightened	*ḍarā huā*
from	*sē*
fruit	*phal*

G

German	*Jarman*
Germany	*Jarmanī*
gift	*tohfā*
give, to	*dēnā*
glass	*gilās*
good (adj)	*achchā*
goodbye	*namastē*
green	*harā*

grey — *salētī*
guide, tour — *tūr gāid*

H

hand (n) — *hātḥ*
handicraft shop — *dastkāri kī dukān*
head — *sīr*
headache — *sīr dard*
hear, to — *sunanā*
heart — *dil*
hello — *namastē*
help, to — *madad karnā*
help! — *madad kījiyē!*
hepatitis — *pīliyā*
here — *yahāñ*
hill — *pahārī*
horse — *ghōrā*
hospital — *aspatāl*
hot — *garam*
hotel — *hōtal*

hour	*ghantā*
how?	*kaisē?*
how many?	*kitnē?*
how much?	*kitnā?*
humid (weather)	*namī*
hundred	*sau*
hungry	*bhūkhā*
hurt, to	*dard hōnā*

I

I	*maiñ*
ice	*barf*
immediately	*jaldī*
immigration office	*imigrēshion aufis*
in	*mēñ*
India	*Bhārat*
Indian	*Bhārtiya*
indigestion	*apach*
injection	*tīkā*
inn	*dharamshālā*

insured (postal article)	*surkshit dak sē*
is (eg he/she/it is)	*hai*
itch	*khujali*

J

Japan	*Japān*
Japanese	*Japānī*
jewellery	*zēvar*
journalist	*patrakār*

K

kerosene	*miṭṭī kā tēl*
key	*chābhī*
kidney	*gurdā*
kilogramme	*kilō*
knife	*chākū*

L

lake	*jhīl*
lamp	*battī*

laundry service	*kapadē dhulnē ki suvidhā*
leave, to	*chalnā*
left, on the	*bāiñ taraf*
leg	*tāñg*
lemon	*nīmbū*
lentils	*dāl*
like, to	*pasañd karnā*
little, a	*kucḥ; thorā*
liver	*jīgar*
load (n)	*bhār*
lock (on door)	*tālā*
long (adj)	*lambā*
loose (clothing)	*dḥīlā*
lose, to	*gumnā*
lost (adj)	*gum honā*
lowest (price)	*kam se kam*
luggage	*sāmān*

M

mail	*dāk*

main street	*mukhya sarak*
malaria	*malēriā*
manager	*prabandhak*
mango	*ām*
many	*bahut*
map	*nakshā*
mark, German (currency)	*Jarman mark*
market	*bāzār*
married	*shādishudā*
matches	*māchīs*
maybe	*shāyad*
meat	*māñs; gosht*
meat balls	*māñs kōftā*
medication	*davā*
meet, to	*milnā*
menstruation	*mahāvārī*
menu	*menyū*
metre	*mītar*
milk	*dūdh*
milk, with	*dūdh kē sāth*

mince	*kīma*
monastery	*maṭh*
money	*paisē*
monkey	*bandar*
more (comparative adj)	*zyādā; adhik*
more (quantity)	*kuch̤ aur*
morning	*subah*
mosque	*masjid*
mosquito	*machḥar*
mosquito net	*macḥardānī*
mosquito repellant	*machrōñ kō bhagānē kī davā*
mountain	*pahārḥ*
movie	*fīlm*
much	*bahut*
mule	*khachhar*
museum	*myūzīam*
music	*sañgīt*
musician	*sangeetkār*
mutton	*bakari yā bḥērḥ ka māñs*

N

name	*nām*
name card (business card)	*parīchaya patra*
near (adj)	*pās*
need, to	*chāhnā*
needle	*sūī*
new	*nayā*
newspaper	*akḥbār*
night	*rāt*
nine	*nau*
nineteen	*unnīs*
ninety	*nabbē*
no	*nahīñ; jī nahīñ*
north	*uttar*
nose	*nāk*
not	*nahīñ*
notes (paper money)	*rupaiyē*
now	*ab*

O

o'clock	*bajē*
office worker	*daftar karmachāri*
old city	*prāchīn shahar*
old: how old are you?	*āpkī kyā umar haiñ?*
one	*ēk*
order (food, etc), to	*mañgvānā*

P

packet	*paket*
pain (medical)	*dard*
Pakistan	*Pākistān*
Pakistani	*Pākistāni*
palace	*mahal*
paper	*kāgaz*
parcel	*pārsal*
park	*bāgīchā; park*
parliament	*sansad bhavan*
passport	*pāspōrt*

patties, vegetable	*sabzi kā samōsā*
pay (money), to	*paisē dēnā*
peak, mountain	*chōṭi*
peas	*maṭar*
pen	*kalam*
penicillin	*pēnisilīn*
pepper	*mīrch*
permitted	*ijāzat*
personal belongings	*nizī chīzeñ*
pharmacy	*davā kī dukān*
piece	*tukrhā*
pillow	*takiyā*
pill (medicine)	*golī*
place	*jagah*
plate	*plēt*
please	*kripyā*
police	*pulis*
police station	*pulis chaukī*
post office	*dāk ghar*
postage stamp	*ḍāk tikat*

postcard	*pōstkārd*
potato	*ālū*
prescription	*doktur kā nuskhā*
printed matter	*likhit sāmagrī*

Q

quality	*kism*
quickly	*jaldī*
quiet (adj)	*shānt*

R

rabies	*jalāntak*
railway station	*rēlwē stēshan*
rain	*bārish*
receipt	*rasīd*
receive (mail), to	*dāk milnā*
red	*lāl*
refreshments	*jalpān*
registered (postal article)	*panjīkrit dāk sē*
rent, room	*kirāyā*

repeat, to	*dōhrānā*
rest, to	*ārām karnā*
restaurant	*bhojanālay*
resting place	*ārām kī jagah*
return, to	*vāpas ānā*
rice	*chāval*
rice, cooked	*pakē huē chāval*
rickshaw	*rikshā*
right, on the	*dāhinī taraf*
river	*nadī*
room	*kamrā*

S

salt	*namak*
sandwich	*sandvich*
second class (rail travel)	*dūsrī shrēnī*
see, to	*dēkhnā*
serious (illness)	*gambhīr*
seven	*sāt*
seventeen	*sattarā*

seventy	*sattar*
sheet	*chādar*
shelter	*sharaṇ*
shirt	*kamīz*
shoe laces	*fītē*
shoes	*jūtē*
shop	*dukān*
shop, handicraft	*dastkāri kī dukānē*
short (length)	*chọtā*
shoulder	*kandhā*
show, to	*dikhānā*
sick	*bīmār*
sightseeing	*darshnīya sthān*
single room	*ēk vyakti kē thaharnē kā kamrā*
sit, to	*baithnā*
six	*chhē*
sixteen	*sōlā*
sixty	*sāṭh*
skirt	*skarṭ*

sleep, to	sōnā
sleeper (railway)	*slīpar*
sleeping bag	*sōnē kā thēlā*
sleeping pill	*sōnē kī gōlī*
slowly	*dhīrē*
small	*chōtā*
snow	*barf*
soap	*sābun*
socks	*mōzē*
something	*kuch*
soup	*shōrbā*
south	*dakshiṇ*
speak, to	*bōlnā*
spicy	*masālēdār*
spinach	*pālak*
spoon	*chammach*
spring (of water)	*jharanā*
stamp, postage	*dāk tikat*
statue	*pratimā*
steal, to	*chōrī karnā*

stomach	*pēt*
stop, to	*ruknā*
stove	*angīthḥī*
straight	*sīdhā*
street	*mārg; sarak*
string	*rassī*
student	*cḥātra*
study, to	*parḥnā*
stuffed pancake	*masālā dōsā*
style (of clothing)	*shēlī*
sugar, with	*chīnī kē sāthḥ*
sunlight; sunny weather	*dhūp*
sweets	*mīthāīyāñ*
Swiss	*Swiss*
Switzerland	*Switzerland*

T

tablet (medicine)	*gōlī*
tailor	*darzī*
take, to	*lēnā*

taxi	*taiksī*
tea	*chāi*
teacher	*adhyāpak*
teashop	*chāi kī dukān*
telephone	*tēlīfōn*
tell, to	*batānā*
temple	*mandir*
ten	*das*
tent	*tambū*
test	*jāñch*
tetanus	*tētnas*
thank you	*dhanyavād*
that	*vah*
that side	*us taraf*
these	*yē*
they	*vē*
thief	*chōr*
thing	*chīz*
third class (rail travel)	*tisrī shrēnī*
thirsty	*pyāsā*

thirteen	*tērah*
thirty	*tīs*
this	*yah*
this side	*is taraf*
those	*vō*
thousand	*ēk hazār*
thread	*dhāgā*
three	*tīn*
throat	*galā*
ticket	*tikat*
ticket office	*tikat ghar*
tight (clothing)	*tañg*
time	*samay*
tip (gratuity)	*bakshish*
tired	*thaka*
today	*āj*
toilet	*shauchālay*
toilet paper	*shauch kā kāgaz*
tomorrow	*kal*
tongue	*jībh*

too	*bahut*
too much (expensive)	*bahut mahẽngā*
too much (quantity)	*bahut zyādā*
tooth	*dā̃t*
tour guide	*tūr gāid*
tourist office	*tūrist aufis*
towel	*tauliyā*
train	*trēn*
train, express	*tēzgāmi gāṛhi*
travellers cheque	*travelers chēk*
twelve	*bārā*
twenty	*bīs*
two	*dō*
typhoid	*āntrajavar*

U

umbrella	*chatrī*
uphill	*ūpar*

V

vegetables	*sabẓīyāñ*
very	*bahut*
very much	*bahut*
village	*gaoñ*

W

wait, to	*intẓār karnā*
wake, to	*jagānā*
want, to	*chāhnā*
water	*pānī*
waterfall	*jal prapāt*
way (path)	*rāstā*
we	*ham*
weather	*mausam*
week, last	*pichhlē saptāh*
week, next	*aglē saptāh*
week, this	*yē saptāh*
west	*pashchim*
what?	*kyā?*

when?	*kab?*
where?	*kahāñ?*
white	*safēd*
who?	*kaun?*
why?	*kyōñ?*
wind	*havā*
with	*kē sāth*
without	*kē binā*

Y

year	*sāl*
yellow	*pīlā*
yes	*hāñ; jī hāñ*
yesterday	*kal*
yet	*abhī*
yoga	*yōgā*
you	*āp*